S0-BYP-244

10/24
STRAND PRICE
$ 5.00

A Tribute to
KENNETH SNELSON

Published on the occasion of the exhibition *A Tribute to Kenneth Snelson*
organized by Marlborough Gallery, New York
September 18 – November 6, 2021

Copyright © 2021 by Dale M. Lanzone, *A Tribute to Kenneth Snelson*
Copyright © 2021 by Marlborough Gallery, New York

All rights reserved. Used with permission.
Photographs by Kenneth Snelson copyright © The Estate of Kenneth Snelson

All rights reserved. No part of this book may be reproduced in any form or by
any electronic or mechanical means, including information storage and retrieval
systems, without permission in writing from the publisher, except by a reviewer
who may quote brief passages in a review.

First Edition

ISBN 978-0-89797-333-5

A Tribute to
KENNETH SNELSON

Essay by Dale M. Lanzone

Photography by Kenneth Snelson

www.marlboroughnewyork.com

Table of Contents

Snelson with *Needle Tower*, Texas, 1968

The intellectual urgency that inspired the Modernists can still be felt in the work of Kenneth Snelson who, for the last five decades, has been engaged in a series of investigations into the structures of nature, the points of convergence between science, mathematics, and art, and the continuity between the micro and macroscopic realms.

Snelson's sculptures create a dynamic equilibrium in which all parts are necessary for the structure to hold. Snelson likes to think of his works as analogues of the larger cosmos where everything is in motion and, in a telling metaphor, he sees the steel or aluminum rods that cross without touching as akin to planets which pass by each other in their orbits without making contact.

Eleanor Heartney
in Kenneth Snelson, *Forces Made Visible*
(Hard Press Editions, 2009)

Snelson at Black Mountain College, 1949

A Tribute to Kenneth Snelson

I first became aware of Kenneth Snelson's structures as sculptures while in graduate school at the California College of the Arts in 1967. At the time I was most interested in objects that were not about something but were in total the thing itself, with minimalism being the contemporary key to that interest. Ken's sculptures were minimal in the sense that they consisted of what was physically necessary to contain a specific structure's tension and compressive energy in a set of formal relationships. To control the combined tension and compressive energies of a structure in order to create a specific design or arrangement of forces was Ken's lifelong intellectual and aesthetic pursuit—to this end, his seminal invention of the patented tensegrity structure at twenty-one years of age was an illustration of his natural genius.

Imagine a twenty-one-year-old Kenneth Snelson arriving at Black Mountain College to study painting with Joseph Albers and, through happenstance, engaging with a young Buckminister Fuller. Together, they develop a soda straw "jitterbug" structure, a precursor to tensegrity. He then goes off on summer vacation and returns to Black Mountain in the autumn with *Wood X-Column*, the first endoskeletal floating-compression structure—what we now call tensegrity structure—a wholly new, uncharted structural system.

To the viewer, the physical magic of a Kenneth Snelson sculpture arises in large part from the weightless gravity-defying character of the metal tubes improbably floating in space, strung between and supported by a complex net of stainless-steel cables. The sculptures are perceptually transfixing in much the same way that the views of the Grand Canyon or across Yosemite Valley to Half Dome are—no interpretation is required to bring the viewer to attention. The back story of Ken's art is extremely interesting and speaks to the very nature and power of invention, but in the end, the physical presence of the works, their otherness and purity of purpose renders them impervious to the abrasive effects of style, fashion, and possibly time itself.

Fuller embraced Ken's invention, called a press conference and announced tensegrity to the world. Now, seventy-three years after Fuller's introduction of tensegrity, Ken's sculptures span the globe with some forty-five monumental structures in important permanent public venues.

Uniquely, Ken became the master of the medium he invented, with his interest in the complex questions surrounding the structure of the universe leading him to engage in ongoing correspondence with quantum physicists and authors such as Isaac Asimov, about Ken's own ideas regarding the underlying structure of the atom. Ken had written extensively on the subject and developed models that gave physical form to an otherwise inconceivable quantum structure at the sub-atomic level. These pursuits both delighted and frustrated Ken; the frustration coming from facing the inherent impossibility of finding a means, outside of mathematics, to represent the fundamental quanta architecture of the universe in the form of visual representation.

Although known primarily for these complex inquiries in sculpture and related patented design technologies, Ken cultivated a body of work in photography that grew out of a lifelong personal connection with the medium. His father, Jack Snelson, realized his dream of owning a camera store in Pendleton, Oregon in 1933, amidst the nadir of the Great Depression. By the mid-thirties his shop was stocked with all of the top-of-the-line brands of the day: Leica, Kodak, Rolleiflex, and Voigtlander. In a few short years the Snelsons had become the resident photographers of Pendleton, with its famous rodeo, the Pendleton Roundup. This childhood familiarity with photographic equipment and processes was stirred on various occasions in the 1970s, upon his encountering vintage cameras at photo-swaps. Ken's New York City panoramas were made using a vintage 1917 16-inch Cirkut camera, one of only thirty ever made.

"Each image is really about my love of New York, an affair that goes back sixty years when I first moved to Manhattan in 1950," Ken wrote in 2011. "Seeing New York as it was thirty or so years ago in these pictures…it's clear that great changes have happened to the face of the city. My aim wasn't especially to make historical records, yet all pictures become so as time passes. My primary interest in all of my panoramas is to discover an unexpected order in reconstructing the location and its geometry, as if to transform an Earth globe into a cartographic projection; a new map of a known landscape."

I always considered Ken's panoramic photographs as investigations into the structure of vision, touching upon how our occipital lobes process and structure visual information. Ken created non-digital photographic images that structure visual data in ways that the occipital lobes cannot. In so doing his panoramas create a somewhat visually disorienting experience as the mind and eye try to understand and meaningfully organize the presented picture.

Over the years I had the pleasure of working with Ken in the development of many exhibitions and large-scale sculptural projects. He loved seeing his sculptures "come to life," a descriptive phrase he often used to define the moment the last tension cable was cinched into place, radiating thousands of pounds of combined compressive/tension energy through every cable and tube. At that moment, the sculpture would fully realize its form, and laden with energy, spring to life.

We had fun and, most of all, interesting times.

Dale M. Lanzone

Snelson with *Arcu Tow*, Wooster Street, New York, 1961

LIST OF PLATES

Snelson with *Sagaponack Weave Pieces*

1. *Tapered X-Column*, 1948-1997
wood and black thread, unique
35 x 6 x 6 in. | 91 x 15.2 x 15.2 cm

Notes:
Snelson constructed this tower of "X-Modules" dated 1948-97, a piece he had
imagined earlier but never built.

2. *Trigonal Tower*, 1962-81
aluminum and stainless-steel cable, edition 2 of 4
65 x 31 ½ x 28 in. | 165.1 x 80 x 71.1 cm

Exhibited:
Kenneth Snelson: Sculpture (2003). Marlborough Gallery, New York, New York. 10 September – 4 October 2003. Reproduced in color, p. 9 (edition not specified).

Kenneth Snelson: Selected Work 1948-2009 (2009). Marlborough Gallery, New York, New York. 19 February – 21 March 2009. Reproduced in color, p. 10 (edition not specified).

Literature:
Kurtz, Stephen A. "Kenneth Snelson: The Elegant Solution." In *Kenneth Snelson*, edited by Bernd Carow, pp. 32-38. Hannover, Germany: Kunstverein Hannover, 1971. Reproduced in black and white, p. 37.

Snelson, Kenneth. *Forces Made Visible*. Lenox, MA: Hard Press Editions, 2009. Reproduced in color, p. 14 (edition not specified).

3. *Needle Tower (model)*, 1968
aluminum and stainless-steel cable, edition 4 of 4
102 x 32 ½ x 38 ½ in. | 259.1 x 82.6 x 97.8 cm

Exhibited:
Kenneth Snelson (1971). Kunstverein Hannover, Hannover, Germany. 13 March – 18 April 1971. Catalogue no. 10; reproduced in black and white, p. 37 (edition not specified).

Kenneth Snelson: The Nature of Structure (1989-90). The New York Academy of Sciences, New York, New York, 31 January – 7 April 1989; traveled to California Museum of Science and Industry, Los Angeles, California, 9 June – 27 August 1989; National Academy of Sciences, Washington, District of Columbia, 5 April – 25 June 1990. Reproduced in black and white, p. 35.

Kenneth Snelson: Sculpture (2003). Marlborough Gallery, New York, New York. 10 September – 4 October 2003. Reproduced in color, p. 9 (edition not specified).

Notes:
This sculpture is a model for a monumental version that was installed at Bryant Park in New York City (1968), and now resides in the collection of the Hirshhorn Museum and Sculpture Garden, Smithsonian Institution, Washington, District of Columbia.

23

4. *V-X*, 1968-1989
aluminum and stainless-steel cable, edition 0 of 4
13 x 21 ½ x 21 ½ in. | 33.0 x 54.6 x 54.6 cm

Exhibited:
Kenneth Snelson: The Nature of Structure (1989-90). The New York Academy of Sciences, New York, New York, 31 January – 7 April 1989; traveled to California Museum of Science and Industry, Los Angeles, California, 9 June – 27 August 1989; National Academy of Sciences, Washington, District of Columbia, 5 April – 25 June 1990. Not reproduced (edition not specified).

Kenneth Snelson (1992). Contemporary Sculpture Center, Tokyo, Japan. 6 February – 7 March 1992. Catalogue no. 5; reproduced in color (edition not specified).

Notes:
This edition was made January 20th, 1989, to travel with the New York Academy of Sciences exhibition. A monumental version of this sculpture is held in the collection of the National Gallery of Art, Washington, District of Columbia.

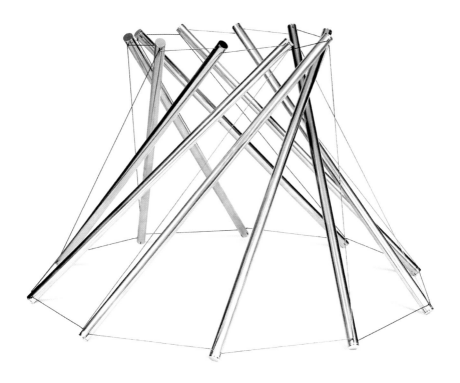

5. *Needle Tower II (Kröller-Müller Tower Model)*, 1969
anodized aluminum and stainless-steel cable, edition 1 of 4
88 x 24 ½ x 24 ½ in. | 223.5 x 62.2 x 62.2 cm

Exhibited:
Kenneth Snelson: Sculptures (1994). Maxwell Davidson Gallery, New York, New York. 19 February – 9 April 1994. Catalogue no. 17; not reproduced (edition not specified).

Notes:
This sculpture is a model for a monumental version held in the collection of the Kröller-Müller Museum, Otterlo, The Netherlands.

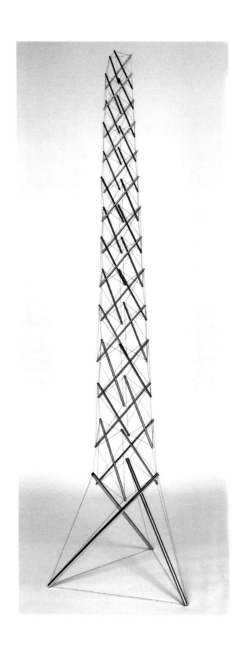

6. *Black E.C. Tower,* 1969-2006
black anodized aluminum upper modules and stainless-steel base module, unique
504 x 132 x 114 in. | 1280.2 x 335.3 x 289.6 cm

Exhibited:
Festival International de Sculpture Contemporaine de Monaco (2000). Monte Carlo, Monaco. 26 June – 31 October 2000.

Deux Américains à Paris: Sculptures de George Rickey et Kenneth Snelson (2006). Jardins du Palais Royal, Paris, France. 23 October – 15 December 2006. Reproduced in color.

Literature:
Snelson, Kenneth. *Forces Made Visible.* Lenox, MA: Hard Press Editions, 2009. Reproduced in color, pp. 88-89 (edition not specified).

Notes:
This work is currently on view on the campus of Pratt Institute, Brooklyn, New York, where it has been installed since 2015.

29

7. *Easy K II*, 1971-2001
aluminum and stainless-steel cable, edition 1 of 4
13 x 77 x 13 in. | 33.0 x 195.6 x 33.0 cm

Exhibited:
Kenneth Snelson: Sculptures (1994). Maxwell Davidson Gallery, New York, New York.
19 February – 9 April 1994. Reproduced in color (edition not specified).

Kenneth Snelson (1995). Contemporary Sculpture Center, Tokyo, Japan. 31 March –
27 May 1995. Catalogue no. 1; reproduced in black and white, pp. 14-15.

Notes:
Monumental versions of this sculpture are held in the collection of Gibbs Farm,
Makarau, New Zealand, and a private collection in Tokyo, Japan.

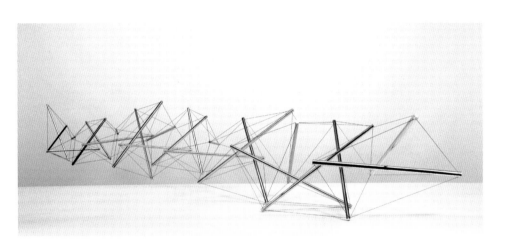

8. *Equilateral Quivering Tower*, 1973-92
chrome-plated brass and stainless-steel cable, edition 2 of 4
102 x 42 x 36 in. | 259.1 x 106.7 x 91.4 cm

Exhibited:
Kenneth Snelson: Sculptures (1994). Maxwell Davidson Gallery, New York, New York.
19 February – 9 April 1994. Reproduced in color (edition not specified).

Kenneth Snelson: Sculpture (2003). Marlborough Gallery, New York, New York.
10 September – 4 October 2003. Reproduced in color, p. 13 (edition not specified).

9. *Black E.C. Tower*, 1974
black anodized aluminum and stainless-steel cable, edition 2 of 4
41 x 14 ½ x 12 ½ in. | 104.1 x 36.8. 31.8 cm

Exhibited:
Kenneth Snelson: Sculptures (1994). Maxwell Davidson Gallery, New York, New York.
19 February – 9 April 1994. Reproduced in color (edition not specified).

Kenneth Snelson: Sculpture (2003). Marlborough Gallery, New York, New York.
10 September – 4 October 2003. Reproduced in color, p. 10.

Literature:
Snelson, Kenneth. *Forces Made Visible.* Lenox, MA: Hard Press Editions, 2009.
Reproduced in black and white, p. 88.

Notes:
The monumental version of this sculpture (cat. no. 6) was exhibited in 2006 at the
Jardins du Palais Royal, Paris, France, and is currently installed on the campus of
Pratt Institute, Brooklyn, New York.

10. *Free Ride Home*, 1974-80
aluminum and stainless-steel cable, edition 3 of 4
23 ¾ x 42 x 35 in. | 60.3 x 106.7 x 88.9 cm

Exhibited:
Kenneth Snelson: The Nature of Structure (1989-90). The New York Academy of Sciences, New York, New York, 31 January – 7 April 1989; traveled to California Museum of Science and Industry, Los Angeles, California, 9 June – 27 August 1989; National Academy of Sciences, Washington, District of Columbia, 5 April – 25 June 1990. Reproduced in black and white, p. 55 (different edition exhibited).

Kenneth Snelson (1992). Contemporary Sculpture Center, Tokyo, Japan. 6 February – 7 March 1992. Catalogue no. 1; reproduced in color (edition not specified).

Kenneth Snelson: Sculpture (2003). Marlborough Gallery, New York, New York. 10 September – 4 October 2003. Reproduced in color, p. 21 (edition not specified).

Literature:
Snelson, Kenneth. *Forces Made Visible.* Lenox, MA: Hard Press Editions, 2009. Reproduced in black and white, p. 78 (edition not specified).

Notes:
A monumental version of this sculpture is held in the collection of Storm King Art Center, Mountainville, New York.

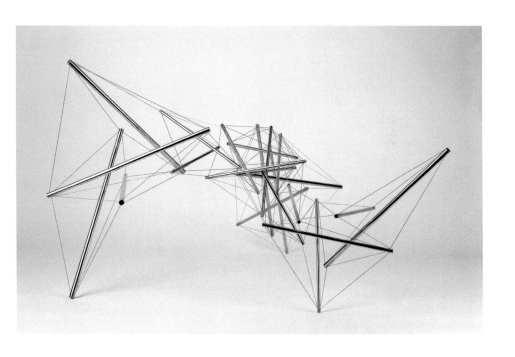

11. *Forest Devil*, 1974-2012
stainless steel, edition 2 of 4
204 x 420 x 300 in. | 518.2 x 1066.8 x 762.0 cm

Exhibited:

Kenneth Snelson (1992). Contemporary Sculpture Center, Tokyo, Japan. 6 February –
7 March 1992. Catalogue no. 3; reproduced in color (edition not specified).

Kenneth Snelson: Sculpture (2003). Marlborough Gallery, New York, New York.
10 September – 4 October 2003. Reproduced in color, p. 23 (edition not specified).

Notes:

Other editions of this sculpture are held in the collections of the Carnegie Museum
of Art, Pittsburgh, Pennsylvania, and the University of Cincinnati Public Art
Collection, Cincinnati, Ohio.

This work is currently on view at Marlborough Sculpture Park, Buchanan, New York.

12. *Sigma Data II*, 1975-92
stainless steel, A.P.
30 x 35 x 21 in. | 76.2 x 88.9 x 53.3 cm

Exhibited:
Kenneth Snelson: Sculptures (1994). Maxwell Davidson Gallery, New York, New York.
19 February – 9 April 1994. Catalogue no. 9; not reproduced (edition not specified).

Kenneth Snelson: Sculpture (2003). Marlborough Gallery, New York, New York.
10 September – 4 October 2003. Reproduced in color, p. 19 (edition not specified).

Literature:
Snelson, Kenneth. *Forces Made Visible.* Lenox, MA: Hard Press Editions, 2009.
Reproduced in color, p. 97 (edition not specified).

13. *Greene Street III*, 1975-93
stainless steel, edition 4 of 4
32 x 27 x 23 in. | 81.3 x 68.6 x 58.4 cm

Exhibited:
Kenneth Snelson (1995). Contemporary Sculpture Center, Tokyo, Japan. 31 March
– 27 May 1995. Catalogue no. 4; reproduced in black and white, p. 18 (edition not
specified).

Kenneth Snelson: Sculpture (2003). Marlborough Gallery, New York, New York.
10 September – 4 October 2003. Reproduced in color, p. 22 (edition not specified).

Literature:
Snelson, Kenneth. *Forces Made Visible*. Lenox, MA: Hard Press Editions, 2009.
Reproduced in color, p. 84 (edition not specified).

14. *Able Charlie*, 1978
aluminum and stainless-steel cable, edition 1 of 4
100 x 106 x 80 in. | 254.0 x 269.2 x 203.2 cm

Exhibited:
Kenneth Snelson (1981-82). Hirshhorn Museum and Sculpture Garden, Smithsonian
Institution, Washington, District of Columbia, 4 June – 9 August 1981; traveled to
Albright-Knox Art Gallery, Buffalo, New York, 12 September – 8 November 1981;
Sarah Campbell Blaffer Gallery, University of Houston, Houston, Texas, 15 January –
21 February 1982. Reproduced in black and white, p. 55 (different version exhibited).

20th Century Sculpture (1999). Nassau County Museum of Art, Roslyn Harbor, New
York. 28 March – 31 May 1999. Reproduced in color, p. 34 (edition not specified).

Literature:
Snelson, Kenneth. *Forces Made Visible*. Lenox, MA: Hard Press Editions, 2009.
Reproduced in black and white, pp. 42-43 (edition not specified).

Notes:
Another edition of this sculpture is held in the collection of the Joslyn Art Museum,
Omaha, Nebraska.

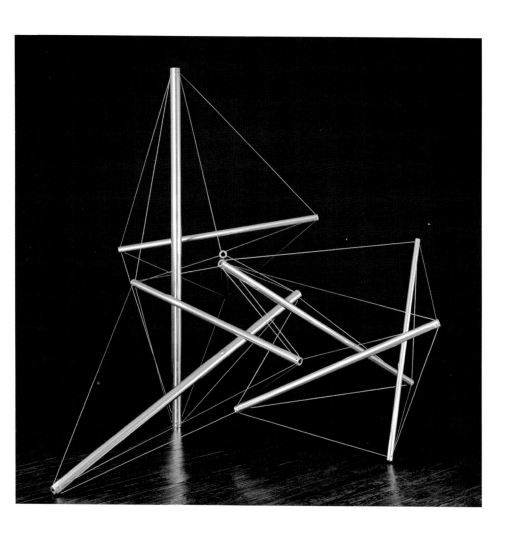

15. *Double Shell Form II*, 1979
aluminum and stainless-steel cable, edition 1 of 4
22 ½ x 22 ½ x 22 ½ in. | 57.1 x 57.1 x 57.1 cm

Literature:
Snelson, Kenneth. *Forces Made Visible*. Lenox, MA: Hard Press Editions, 2009.
Reproduced in color, p. 106 (edition not specified).

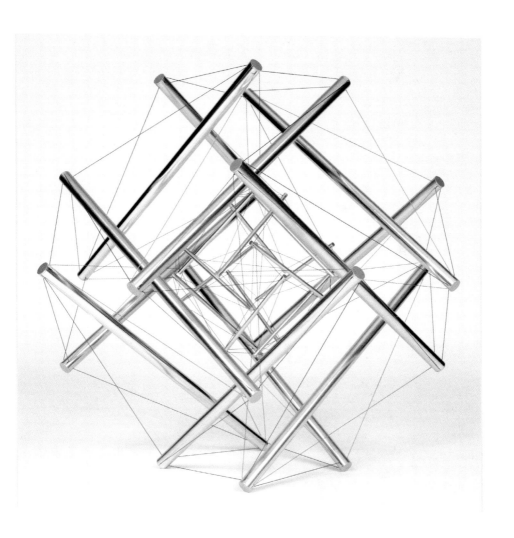

16. *Flat Out*, 1979
stainless steel, edition 3 of 4
16 x 20 x 11 in. | 40.6 x 50.8 x 27.9 cm

Exhibited:
Kenneth Snelson (1995). Contemporary Sculpture Center, Tokyo, Japan. 31 March
– 27 May 1995. Catalogue no. 2; reproduced in black and white, p. 16 (edition not
specified).

Kenneth Snelson: Sculpture (2003). Marlborough Gallery, New York, New York.
10 September – 4 October 2003. Reproduced in color, p. 29 (edition not specified).

Literature:
Snelson, Kenneth. *Forces Made Visible*. Lenox, MA: Hard Press Editions, 2009.
Reproduced in color, p. 99 (edition not specified).

17. *Tallstar*, 1979
aluminum and stainless-steel cable, edition 6 of 6
27 ¾ x 19 ½ x 18 in. | 70.5 x 49.5 x 45.7 cm

Exhibited:
Kenneth Snelson (1992). Contemporary Sculpture Center, Tokyo, Japan. 6 February –
7 March 1992. Catalogue no. 2; reproduced in color (edition not specified).

Kenneth Snelson: Sculptures (1994). Maxwell Davidson Gallery, New York, New York.
19 February – 9 April 1994. Catalogue no. 14; not reproduced (edition not specified).

MathArt/ArtMath (2002). Selby Gallery, Ringling School of Art and Design, Sarasota,
Florida. 22 February – 30 March 2002.

A Black Mountain Assemblage (2004). ACA Galleries, New York, New York. 20 March –
10 April 2004. No catalogue produced.

Literature:
Snelson, Kenneth. *Forces Made Visible.* Lenox, MA: Hard Press Editions, 2009.
Reproduced in black and white, p. 56 (edition not specified).

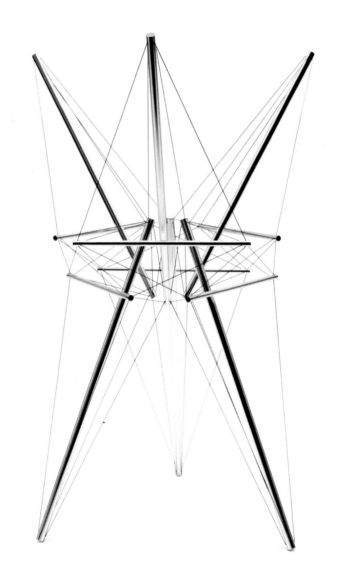

51

18. *Four Chances*, 1979
aluminum and stainless-steel cable, edition 4 of 4
35 x 41 x 31 in. | 88.9 x 104.1 x 78.7 cm

Exhibited:
Kenneth Snelson (1981-82). Hirshhorn Museum and Sculpture Garden, Smithsonian Institution, Washington, District of Columbia, 4 June – 9 August 1981; traveled to Albright-Knox Art Gallery, Buffalo, New York, 12 September – 8 November 1981; Sarah Campbell Blaffer Gallery, University of Houston, Houston, Texas, 15 January – 21 February 1982. Reproduced in black and white, p. 56.

Kenneth Snelson (1992). Contemporary Sculpture Center, Tokyo, Japan. 6 February – 7 March 1992. Catalogue no. 4; reproduced in color.

Kenneth Snelson: Sculpture (2003). Marlborough Gallery, New York, New York. 10 September – 4 October 2003. Reproduced in color, p. 20.

Literature:
Snelson, Kenneth. *Forces Made Visible*. Lenox, MA: Hard Press Editions, 2009. Reproduced in color, p. 101 (edition not specified).

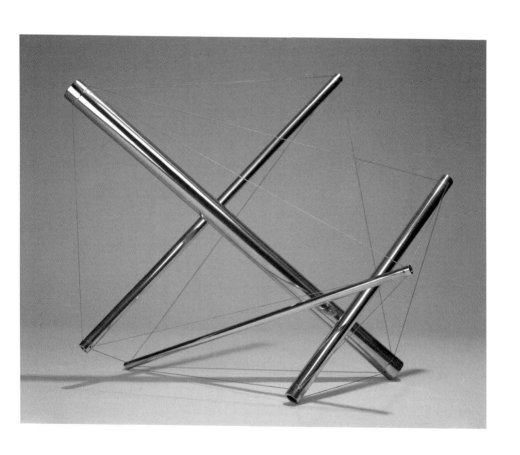

19. *Mozart I*, 1981-82
stainless steel, edition 2 of 4
35 x 44 x 43 in. | 88.9 x 111.8 x 109.2 cm

Exhibited:
Kenneth Snelson (1992). Contemporary Sculpture Center, Tokyo, Japan. 6 February –
7 March 1992. Catalogue no. 13; reproduced in color (edition not specified).

Kenneth Snelson: Sculptures (1994). Maxwell Davidson Gallery, New York, New York.
19 February – 9 April 1994. Reproduced in color (edition not specified).

Kenneth Snelson: Selected Work 1948-2009 (2009). Marlborough Chelsea, New York,
New York. 19 February – 21 March 2009. Reproduced in color, p. 17 (edition not
specified).

Literature:
Snelson, Kenneth. *Forces Made Visible*. Lenox, MA: Hard Press Editions, 2009.
Reproduced in black and white and color, pp. 80-81 (different version reproduced).

20. *B-Tree II*, 1981-2008
stainless steel, unique
108 x 114 x 130 in. | 274.3 x 289.6 x 330.2 cm

Exhibited:
Kenneth Snelson: Sculpture (2003). Marlborough Gallery, New York, New York.
10 September – 4 October 2003. Reproduced in color, p. 8 (edition not specified).

Kenneth Snelson: Selected Work 1948-2009 (2009). Marlborough Chelsea, New York, New York. 19 February – 21 March 2009. Reproduced in color, p. 18 (edition not specified).

7 World Trade Center (2012). Lobby installation, New York, New York. 28 March – 12 June 2012. No catalogue produced.

Large Sculptures (2016). Marlborough Gallery, New York, New York. 7 April – 7 May 2016. Reproduced in color, p. 29 (edition not specified).

Literature:
Snelson, Kenneth. *Forces Made Visible*. Lenox, MA: Hard Press Editions, 2009. Reproduced in color, p. 77 (different version reproduced).

Notes:
A monumental version of this sculpture is held in the collection of the Frederik Meijer Gardens and Sculpture Park, Grand Rapids, Michigan. A second variation is held in the collection of the National Science Foundation, Washington, District of Columbia.

21. *Corner of Chambers and Greenwich Streets*, 1979
gelatin silver print, edition 2 of 5
15 ½ x 70 ½ in. | 39.4 x 179.1 cm

Exhibited:
Kenneth Snelson: New York City Panoramas (2011). Marlborough Gallery, New York,
New York. 30 March – 23 April 2011. Reproduced in black and white.

22. *Sixth Avenue/Exxon Building*, 1979
gelatin silver print, A.P.
15 ½ x 83 in. | 39.4 x 210.8 cm

Literature:
Burrows, Joelle. *Kenneth Snelson: The Nature of Structure.* New York: New York Academy
of Sciences, 1989. Reproduced in black and white, pp. 45-46.

23. *East River Drive Under Brooklyn Bridge*, 1980
gelatin silver print, edition 4 of 10
15 ½ x 112 in. | 39.4 x 284.5 cm

Exhibited:

Kenneth Snelson (1981-82). Hirshhorn Museum and Sculpture Garden, Smithsonian
Institution, Washington, District of Columbia, 4 June – 9 August 1981; traveled to
Albright-Knox Art Gallery, Buffalo, New York, 12 September – 8 November 1981;
Sarah Campbell Blaffer Gallery, University of Houston, Houston, Texas, 15 January –
21 February 1982. Reproduced in black and white, p. 70.

24. *Parking Lot, Mercer and Grand Streets*, 1980
gelatin silver print, edition 2 of 10
15 ½ x 100 in. | 39.4 x 254.0 cm

Exhibited:
Kenneth Snelson (1981-82). Hirshhorn Museum and Sculpture Garden, Smithsonian
Institution, Washington, District of Columbia, 4 June – 9 August 1981; traveled to
Albright-Knox Art Gallery, Buffalo, New York, 12 September – 8 November 1981;
Sarah Campbell Blaffer Gallery, University of Houston, Houston, Texas, 15 January –
21 February 1982. Reproduced in black and white, p. 70.

25. *Times Square*, 1980
gelatin silver print, edition 1 of 15
15 ½ x 109 ½ in. | 39.4 x 278.1 cm

Exhibited:
Kenneth Snelson: New York City Panoramas (2011). Marlborough Gallery, New York,
New York. 30 March – 23 April 2011. Reproduced in black and white.

Literature:
Snelson, Kenneth. *Forces Made Visible*. Lenox, MA: Hard Press Editions, 2009.
Reproduced in black and white, p. 161 (edition not specified).

KENNETH SNELSON

1927
Born in Pendleton, Oregon

2016
Died in New York, New York

Education

1946-1951 —
Studied at Black Mountain College, Black Mountain, North Carolina; Chicago
Institute of Design, Chicago, Illinois; University of Oregon, Eugene, Oregon; and
with Fernand Léger in Paris, France

SOLO EXHIBITIONS

2011
Kenneth Snelson: New York City Panoramas, Marlborough Gallery, New York, New York

2009
Kenneth Snelson, Selected Work: 1948-2009, Marlborough Chelsea, New York, New York

2003
Kenneth Snelson: Sculpture, Marlborough Gallery, New York, New York
Large Scale Panoramas, Laurence Miller Gallery, New York, New York

1999
Kenneth Snelson: Sculptures and Drawings 1968-1998, Marlborough Chelsea, New York,
New York

1998
Maxwell Davidson Gallery, New York, New York

1995
Contemporary Sculpture Center, Tokyo

1994
Maxwell Davidson Gallery, New York, New York
Anderson Gallery, Buffalo, New York
Laurence Miller Gallery, New York, New York

1993
Yoh Art Gallery, Osaka, Japan

1992
Kenneth Snelson, Contemporary Sculpture Center, Tokyo, Japan

1991
Yoh Art Gallery, Osaka, Japan

1990
New York Academy of Sciences, New York, New York
National Academy of Sciences, Washington, District of Columbia
Zabriskie Gallery, New York, New York

1986
Zabriskie Gallery, New York, New York; traveled to Zabriskie Gallery, Paris, France

1984
deCordova Sculpture Park and Museum, Lincoln, Massachusetts

1982
Kenneth Snelson, Blaffer Gallery, The Art Museum of the University of Houston, Houston, Texas

1981
Hirshhorn Museum and Sculpture Garden, Washington, District of Columbia
Kenneth Snelson, Albright-Knox Art Gallery, Buffalo, New York
Zabriskie Gallery, New York, New York

1977
Nationalgalerie, Berlin, Germany
Wilhelm Lehmbruck Museum, Duisburg, Germany

1971
Kenneth Snelson, Kunstverein Hannover, Hannover, Germany

1970
Kunsthalle, Düsseldorf, Germany

1969
Rijksmuseum Kröller-Müller, Otterlo, The Netherlands

1968
Bryant Park, New York, New York

1966
Dwan Gallery, Los Angeles, California

SELECTED GROUP EXHIBITIONS

2016
Large Sculptures, Marlborough Gallery, New York, New York

2012
Atlanta Botanical Gardens, Atlanta, Georgia

2011
Constructivists: George Rickey and Kenneth Snelson, Marlborough Gallery, New York, New York

2008
Geometry as Image, Robert Miller Gallery, New York, New York
Digital Stone Exhibition, Today Art Museum, Beijing, China

2006
Sculptures de George Rickey et Kenneth Snelson: Deux Américains à Paris, Jardins du Palais Royal, Paris, France

2002
Marlborough Gallery, New York, New York

1999
Stamford Outdoor Sculpture Exhibition, Stamford, Connecticut
Neuberger Biennial Exhibition of Public Art, Purchase, New York
20th Century Sculpture, Nassau County Museum of Art, Roslyn Harbor, New York

1995
Japan, U.S., Photography, Takashimaya Gallery, New York, New York

1987
The Arts at Black Mountain College, Grey Art Gallery, New York, New York

1983
Big Pictures, The Museum of Modern Art, New York, New York

1980
Hayward Gallery, London, England

1979
Albright-Knox Gallery, Buffalo, New York

1971
Sonsbeek '71, Arnhem, The Netherlands

1970
Sammlung Etzold, Kolnischer Kunstverein, Cologne, Germany
Salon International de Galeries Pilotes, Lausanne, Switzerland

1969
Twentieth Century Art from the Rockefeller Collection, The Museum of Modern Art,
New York, New York

1968
Prospect '68, Düsseldorf, Germany

1967
Sculpture of the Sixties, Los Angeles County Museum of Art, Los Angeles, California

1966
Sculpture Annual, Whitney Museum of American Art, New York, New York

SELECTED AWARDS

2002
The Elizabeth N. Watrous Gold Medal, The National Academy Museum and School of Fine Arts, New York, New York

2001
Civic Environment Award, City of Osaka, Osaka, Japan

1999
Biennial Honoree, Neuberger Museum of Art, Purchase College, State University of New York, Purchase, New York
Lifetime Achievement Award, International Sculpture Center, Hamilton, New Jersey

Snelson with *Planar Pc*, Spring Street, New York, 1961

Snelson with *Packed Network*, Central Park, New York

1994
Membership, The American Academy of Arts and Letters, New York, New York

1991
Award, The American Institute of Architects Kansas City Chapter, Kansas City, Missouri

1989
Prix Ars Electronica, Ars Electronica, Linz, Austria

1987
Art Award, The American Academy of Arts and Letters, New York, New York

1985
Honorary Doctorate, School of Humanities, Arts, and Social Sciences, Rensselaer Polytechnic Institute, Troy, New York

1981
Award, The American Institute of Architects (AIA), Washington, District of Columbia

1976
DAAD Fellowship, Berlin Künstlerprogramm, Berlin, Germany

1974
Award for Sculpture, Reynolds Metals Company, Richmond, Virginia
Grant, National Endowment for the Arts, Washington, District of Columbia
Iowa City Sculpture Competition, Iowa City, Iowa
Advisory Board, The Public Arts Fund, New York, New York

1971
Award for Sculpture, New York State Council on the Arts, New York, New York

LIST OF COLLECTIONS

Addison Gallery of American Art, Andover, Massachusetts
Albright-Knox Art Gallery, Buffalo, New York
Art Institute of Chicago, Chicago, Illinois
Asheville Art Museum, Asheville, North Carolina
Australian National Gallery, Canberra, Australia
Birmingham Museum of Art, Birmingham, Alabama
Brooklyn Museum, Brooklyn, New York
Cantor Center for Visual Arts, Stanford University, Stanford, Connecticut
Carnegie Museum of Art, Pittsburgh, Pennsylvania
City of Baltimore, Maryland
City of Buffalo, New York
City of Hamburg, Germany
City of Hannover, Germany
City of Iowa City, Iowa
City of San Diego, California
Cleveland Museum of Art, Cleveland, Ohio
Columbus Museum of Art, Columbus, Ohio
Dallas Museum of Fine Arts, Dallas, Texas
deCordova Sculpture Park and Museum, Lincoln, Massachusetts
Frederik Meijer Gardens and Sculpture Park, Grand Rapids, Michigan
Gibbs Farm, Kaipara, New Zealand
Hallmark, Inc., Kansas City, Missouri
Hirshhorn Museum and Sculpture Garden, Washington, District of Columbia
Hunter Museum of Art, Chattanooga, Tennessee
Kröller-Müller Museum, Otterlo, The Netherlands
Metropolitan Museum of Art, New York, New York
Miami-Dade Art in Public Spaces, Miami, Florida
Milwaukee Art Institute, Milwaukee, Wisconsin
Musée de Grenoble, Grenoble, France
Museum of Modern Art, New York, New York
New Jersey State Museum, Trenton, New Jersey
New Orleans Museum of Art, New Orleans, Louisiana

Northwood Institute, Dallas, Texas
Neuberger Museum of Art, Purchase College, State University of New York, Purchase, New York
Osaka Prefecture University, Osaka, Japan
Portland Art Museum, Portland, Oregon
Princeton University Art Museum, Princeton, New Jersey
Rockefeller Estate, Pocantico Hills, New York
San Diego Community College, San Diego, California
San Francisco Museum of Modern Art, San Francisco, California
Shiga Museum of Modern Art, Shiga, Japan
Smithsonian Museum of American Art, Washington, District of Columbia
Snite Museum of Art, University of Notre Dame, Notre Dame, Indiana
Speed Art Museum, Louisville, Kentucky
St. Bride's Farm, Upperville, Virginia
Stanford University, Palo Alto, California
Stedelijk Museum, Amsterdam, The Netherlands
Storm King Art Center, Mountainville, New York
University of Cincinnati, Cincinnati, Ohio
University of Michigan, Ann Arbor, Michigan
Wakayama Museum of Art, Wakayama, Japan
Walker Art Center, Minneapolis, Minnesota
Whitney Museum of American Art, New York, New York
Wilhelm Lehmbruck Museum, Duisburg, Germany

SELECTED BIBLIOGRAPHY

Ashton, Dore. "Historicism and Respect for Tradition." *Studio International* 171, no. 878 (1966): 275-279.

Burnham, Jack. *Beyond Modern Sculpture: The Effects of Science and Technology on the Sculpture of the Century.* New York: George Braziller, 1989.

Burrows, Joelle. *Kenneth Snelson: The Nature of Structure.* New York: New York Academy of Sciences, 1989.

Busch, Julia M. *A Decade of Sculpture: The New Media in the 1960s.* Philadelphia: The Art Alliance Press; Associated University Presses: London, 1974.

Canaday, John. "Kenneth Snelson Shows Influence of Fuller." *The New York Times.* April 16, 1966.

Heartney, Eleanor. *Kenneth Snelson: Art and Ideas.* Web Publication: Kenneth Snelson, 2013.

Kurtz, Stephen A. "Kenneth Snelson: The Elegant Solution." *Art News.* October 1968.

Muller, Gregoire. "Kenneth Snelson's Position is Unique." In *Kenneth Snelson.* Hannover: Kunstverein Hannover, 1971.

Snelson, Kenneth. Interview by Angela Schneider. *Kenneth Snelson.* Berlin: Nationalgalerie, 1977.

Snelson, Kenneth. *Kenneth Snelson: Forces Made Visible.* Lenox, MA: Hard Press Editions, 2009.

Struycken, Peter. Catalogue essay. In *Kenneth Snelson.* Otterlo, The Netherlands: Rijksmuseum Kröller-Müller, 1969.

Tuchman, Maurice. *American Sculpture of the Sixties.* Los Angeles: Los Angeles County Museum of Art, 1967.

Wieder, Laurance. *Full Circle: Panoramas by Kenneth Snelson.* New York: Aperature Foundation, 1990.

Snelson with *Arc Joint*, New York World's Fair, New York, 1964

MARLBOROUGH NEW YORK
545 WEST 25TH STREET
NEW YORK, NY 10001
212 541 4900

DOUGLAS KENT WALLA, CEO — dkwalla@marlboroughgallery.com

SEBASTIAN SARMIENTO, Director — sarmiento@marlboroughgallery.com
NICOLE SISTI, Assistant to Sebastian Sarmiento — sisti@marlboroughgallery.com

DIANA BURROUGHS, Director — burroughs@marlboroughgallery.com
REN PAN, Assistant to Diana Burroughs — pan@marlboroughgallery.com

ALEXA BURZINSKI, Associate Director — burzinski@marlboroughgallery.com

MEGHAN BOYLE KIRTLEY, Administrator — boyle@marlboroughgallery.com
GREG O'CONNOR, Comptroller — greg@marlboroughgallery.com
DiBOMBA KAZADI, Bookkeeper — kazadi@marlboroughgallery.com

AMY CAULFIELD, Registrar — caulfield@marlboroughgallery.com
BIANCA CLARK, Registrar — clark@marlboroughgallery.com

LUKAS HALL, Archivist — hall@marlboroughgallery.com
MARISSA MOXLEY, Archivist — moxley@marlboroughgallery.com

SARAH GICHAN, Gallery Assistant — gichan@marlboroughgallery.com

JOHN WILLIS, Warehouse Manager — willis@marlboroughgallery.com

ANTHONY NICI, Master Crater — nici@marlboroughgallery.com
JEFF SERINO, Exhibition Coordinator — serino@marlboroughgallery.com
PETER PARK, Exhibition Coordinator — park@marlboroughgallery.com
MATT CASTILLO, Preparator — mnywarehouse@marlboroughgallery.com

MARLBOROUGH FINE ART (LONDON)
6 ALBEMARLE STREET
MAYFAIR
LONDON W1S 4BY
UNITED KINGDOM
+44 20 7629 5161

JOE BALFOUR, Head of Graphics	balfour@marlboroughgallery.com
JULIE BLEAS, Gallery Assistant / Digital	bleas@marlboroughgallery.com
KATE CHIPPERFIELD, Sales / Graphics Registrar	chipperfield@marlboroughgallery.com
HARRY CODAY, Gallery Assistant	coday@marlboroughgallery.com
TOMMY DOUGLAS, Gallery Technician	douglas@marlboroughgallery.com
JESSICA DRAPER, Sales Director	draper@marlboroughgallery.com
JOHN ERLE-DRAX, Chairman	erle-drax@marlboroughgallery.com
ASHLEY GOMA, Senior Registrar	goma@marlboroughgallery.com
LAURA LANGELUDDECKE, Executive Assistant to Directors and Researcher	langeluddecke@marlboroughgallery.com
NINA LEDWOCH, Gallery Assistant / Front of House	ledwoch@marlboroughgallery.com
DEBORAH LOWE, Accounts Assistant	lowe@marlboroughgallery.com
MARY MILLER, Director	miller@marlboroughgallery.com
GEOFFREY PARTON, Director	parton@marlboroughgallery.com
FRANKIE ROSSI, Managing Director	rossi@marlboroughgallery.com
ANGELA TREVATT, Senior Bookkeeper / Finance and Administrative Executive	trevatt@marlboroughgallery.com
WILL WRIGHT, Associate Director	wright@marlboroughgallery.com

GALERÍA MARLBOROUGH MADRID
ORFILA, 5
28010 MADRID
SPAIN
+34 91 319 1414

ANNE BARTHE, Sales Director — abarthe@galeriamarlborough.com
BELÉN HERRERA OTTINO, Sales Director — bherrera@galeriamarlborough.com
CLAUDIA MANZANO, Sales — cmanzano@galeriamarlborough.com
NEREA PÉREZ, Press, Auctions — nperez@galeriamarlborough.com
NIEVES RUBIÑO, Director of Finance, Legal and HR — nrubino@galeriamarlborough.com
GERMÁN LUCAS, Finance Assistant — glucas@galeriamarlborough.com
CYNTHIA GONZÁLEZ, Registrar — cgonzalez@galeriamarlborough.com
JARA HERRANZ, Catalogues, Archives — jherranz@galeriamarlborough.com
NOEMÍ MORENA, Reception — nmorena@galeriamarlborough.com
FERMÍN ROSADO, Warehouse — frosado@galeriamarlborough.com
JUAN GARCÍA, Warehouse — jgarcia@galeriamarlborough.com

GALERÍA MARLBOROUGH BARCELONA
C/ ENRIC GRANADOS, 68
08008 BARCELONA
+34 93 467 44 54

MERCEDES ROS, Director, Sales, Public Relation — mros@galeriamarlborough.com
LAURA RODRÍGUEZ, Registrar, Press, Sales, Reception — lrodriguez@galeriamarlborough.com
ESTER GARCÍA, Catalogues, Press, Reception — eguntin@galeriamarlborough.com

Snelson with 16-inch Cirkut camera, New York, 1997

Editors: Diana Burroughs, Lukas Hall, and Marissa Jade Moxley

Design: Dana Martin-Strebel

Edition of 1000
Printed in China by Permanent Press

$14.95
ISBN 978-0-89797-333-5
51495>

9 780897 973335